What's So Striking About lightning?

And Other Questions about...
The Weather

Roger

Howerton

Master
Books

Can a Groundhog Really Predict the Weather?

Although it is not a legally recognized holiday in the United States, Groundhog Day occurs on February 2 each year. (Most *groundhogs* don't even get the day off.) It is said that if a groundhog does not see its shadow, it will remain above ground, signaling the end of winter. If it does see its shadow, it will be frightened and return into its burrow signifying that winter will continue for six more weeks. Of course, a groundhog can't predict the weather any better than a meteorologist, and, technically, spring always arrives on or near March 21, whether a groundhog, badger, meteorologist, or anybody else sees his shadow.

I'm Glad He Doesn't Work for the National Weather Service:

Over the past 60 years or so, the "official" groundhog at Puxatawny, Pennsylvania has predicted the arrival of spring-like weather correctly less than 30% of the time.

Herbal Weatherman:

The scales of pine cones will close when rain is on the way. Dandelion blooms will also close.

Forecast for Mexico:

Chili today and hot tamale!

Ask Max!

Space Weatherman:

"Ring around the moon, rain coming soon" is fairly accurate because cirrus clouds often precede low-pressure systems, and the icy clouds reflect the light of the moon.

Bible Weatherman:

"He answered and said unto them, When it is evening, ye say, It will be fair weather: for the sky is red. And in the morning, It will be foul weather to day: for the sky is red and lowring" (Matt. 16:2,3).

Insect Weatherman:

It is agreed that you can tell the temperature by counting the number of chirps from a cricket. The exact formula is in debate, however. Most people use this simple formula to arrive at the approximate temperature: Count the number of chirps a cricket makes in 15 seconds, and then add 40.

Can Fog Kill People?

Let's first consider what fog is and what causes it. Simply put, a fog is a cloud near the ground. The air around us always holds some moisture. Warm air can hold more moisture than cold air. When a warm mass of air comes into contact with a cold mass, the warm air will cool. Since it has cooled, it cannot hold all of the moisture that it held as warm air. The water molecules will condense (change into a liquid), forming fog. The droplets of water that make up the fog (or even a cloud in the sky) rest on the dust molecules in the air, and are light enough to remain suspended.

Fog may stay around for a few hours or for many days. Usually, it is dissipated (broken up) by the wind or the heat of the sun.

Foggy Mountain Breakdown:

Fog, depending upon its thickness, makes visibility very difficult, even to the point of hazard. Lighthouses and foghorns are used to prevent boats from crashing into the shore or each other. Many accidents occur on the highways because of dense fog. Beyond that, smoke from places of industry and exhaust fumes from cars can mix with the fog causing "smog." The poisonous particles in the smog can kill people because there is no oxygen in the air for people to breathe. These are commonly called "killer fogs."

Ask Max!

Q. What do you see in California when the fog lifts?

A. UCLA.

Killer Fogs:

December, 1930: Caused by various industries, a killer fog settles in the Meuse Valley in Belgium, killing 63 and causing another 600 to be ill. The major toxin in the fog was sulfur dioxide.

October 26-31, 1948: Twenty people die and over 7,000 are hospitalized in Donora, Pennsylvania. The killer fog was caused by pollutants from a steel mill, sulfuric acid plant, and a zinc production plant.

December 4-8, 1952: London, England is held in the grip of the worst killer fog ever reported. Weather conditions were perfect for the toxic fog to linger in the city, trapped between the surrounding hills and the warm air above it. The fog was so thick that vehicles had to use headlights in the daytime, and buses would only run with a guide walking ahead. Eventually, all mechanical transportation in the city except the subway came to a halt. As many as four thousand people died.

November 8-17, 1953: New York City is blanketed in smog for ten straight days, resulting in 200 deaths.

It's true that there is often a smell before and after a rain, but it is not the water that people smell. The smells can come from different sources. One odor is actually caused by bacteria, and will be noticeable in the country, especially near forests. These certain bacteria grow in the damp soil on the forest floor. As the soil dries out, the bacteria produce spores in the soil. When it rains, the raindrops beat the soil and drive the spores upward into the moist air, which easily carries them aloft. It is actually the sweet smell of these spores that we smell. You will notice an even stronger fragrance after a long dry spell.

Another source of a pleasant rain smell is from oils released by vegetation. The moist air carries the scent from these fragrant oils.

Unpleasant rain odors can be caused from pollutants in the air and on the ground.

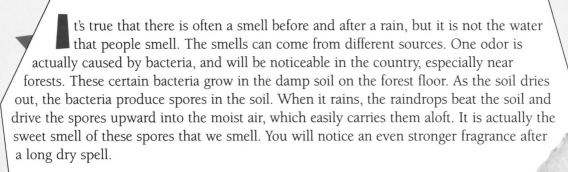

Cold Front

Warm Front

A Foot Will Make It Knee-Deep:

On June 22, 1947, 12 inches (304.8 mm) of rain fell in 42 minutes at Holt, Missouri, setting a new world record for the most rain in the least amount of time.

A thunderstorm generally occurs when a cold front runs into a warm air front.

Ask Max!

Q. Why didn't Noah play cards on the ark?

A. Mrs. Noah sat on the deck!

How Much Is an Inch of Rain?

One inch of rain falling on one acre is equal to about 27,154 gallons of water.

Probably Didn't Want to Get It Wet:

Umbrellas were first used by the ancient Chinese and Egyptians as protection from the sun. The Romans were the first to use them to keep dry.

The Rain in Spain . . . and Everywhere Else:

The Bible records that once, because of man's wickedness, God decided He would destroy the earth and begin again. God gave men and women a chance to repent and obey Him, but they didn't. Only Noah and his family obeyed God.

Rain fell for 40 days and 40 nights. Not only rain, but great floods of water spewed out of the earth and out of the sky. This was more than just a lot of rain — it was total destruction of the planet. God preserved the animals and Noah's family inside of the ark. They lived in the ark exactly one year and ten days waiting for the water to go down and the earth to dry (Gen. 7:11-8:16).

Does It Ever Rain Cats and Dogs?

The old phrase "it's raining cats and dogs," signifying a downpour of rain, dates back to . . . well, no one really knows how far back it goes, or where it came from. The earliest mention of the phrase may have been in Jonathan Swift's *Polite Conversation* in 1708. It was probably a common saying long before then.

The suction from tornadoes can pick up objects (including live ones) and pull them into the clouds, from which they may later fall in a different location. Though there are no records of literal rains of cats and dogs, it has rained other strange things.

Shell We Dents?

A thunderstorm was in full swing near Vicksburg, Mississippi in May of 1894 and hail was falling. One hailstone that fell that day was huge. Ice had formed around a turtle in the cloud before it came down with the other hailstones.

Q. What do you get after it rains cats and dogs?

A. Mud poodles!

Look! Up in the Sky!

Kansas City, Missouri received a rain of frogs that blanketed the city on July 12, 1873.

I've Seen Fire and I've Seen Rain:

In Genesis Chapter 19, the Bible tells us that God rained down fire and brimstone from out of the sky on the wicked cities of Sodom and Gomorrah. This story reminds us that God is holy, and He hates sin.

But What About the Box Springs?

A tornado in Worcester, Massachusetts in June of 1953 carried pieces of mattresses into the thunder-storm and coated them in ice. The icy chunks of mattress rained down in Boston Harbor over 40 miles away.

'Eeling Mighty Fine:

In May of 1892, eels rained from the sky along with the rain in Coalburg, Alabama. Farmers who lived nearby brought carts into town and carried the dead eels off to use as fertilizer.

Q. What's worse than raining cats and dogs?

A. Hailing taxis!

Does Lightning Ever Strike Twice in the Same Place?

When you understand that lightning strikes the earth over three billion times a year, then it is easy to see that it has to strike twice in the same place at some time or another. In fact, lightning may strike the same object several times during the same thunderstorm.

A Striking Statistic:

Lightning strikes somewhere on the earth around 6,000 times every minute.

King Kong Slept Here:

Lightning always seeks the shortest route to the ground, and anything in contact with the ground makes that route even shorter for lightning. This means that the taller an object is, the more likely it is to be hit by lightning. The Empire State Building is struck by lightning about 100 times per year. It serves as a lightning rod for its surrounding area in New York City.

Ask Max!

Human Lightning Rod:

Although lightning, on the average, kills more people each year than tornadoes, many people survive lightning strikes. The world record for being struck the most times by lightning is held by park ranger Roy Sullivan of Virginia, who was struck by lightning seven times within 35 years. According to the *Guinness Book of Records*, Sullivan was first hit by lightning in 1942, knocking his big toenail off. Beginning in 1969, the next six lightning strikes burned off his eyebrows, knocked him unconscious, seared his left shoulder, ripped through his hat, set his hair on fire twice (the first time, he dumped a bucket of water over his head to put out the fire), threw him out of his truck, knocked his left shoe off, injured his ankle, and burned his stomach and chest.

Q. What did Benjamin Franklin say when he discovered electricity?

A. Nothing — he was too shocked!

Rain, Rain Go Away:

At any given moment, there are 1,800 thunder-storms in progress somewhere on the earth.

Lotsa Lightning:

The U. S. government monitors an average of 25 million strokes of lightning from the cloud to the ground every year in the United States.

Because light travels faster than sound, you can estimate the distance from where you are to the lightning strike by counting the number of seconds between the lightning flash and the thunder's boom and then dividing by five. For example, if the number of seconds between the lightning and the thunder is ten, then the lightning struck two miles away.

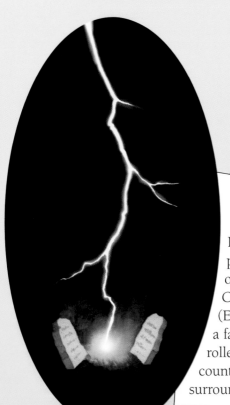

Let There Be Lightning,

In the Bible, lightning is symbolic of the awesome power of God and His angels. Lightning was seen on Mount Sinai shortly before the Ten Commandments were given to Moses from God (Ex. 19:16). Daniel saw in a vision an angel with a face like lightning (Dan. 10:6). The angel that rolled the stone away from Christ's tomb had a countenance like lightning (Matt. 28:3). Lightning surrounds the throne of God (Rev. 4:5).

Man Alive!

Eighty-five percent of the people killed by lightning are male.

What Are the Odds?

According to the National Oceanic and Atmospheric Association's National Weather Service, the average annual number of deaths by lightning in the United States is 90. Putting together their other statistics, you have a greater chance of getting struck by lightning if you are a male, in Florida, in July, on a Sunday around 4 p.m. You might also do well to stay out of Texas and North Carolina if you attract electricity!

Truth Is Stranger Than Fiction:

The BBC reports that in October of 1998, during a soccer game in the eastern Kasai Province of the Democratic Republic of Congo, Africa, a single bolt of lightning killed all 11 members of the visiting team. The home team was left unscathed, leading local people to wonder if a curse had been placed on the unfortunate team. The score was tied 1 – 1 when the lightning struck.

How Fast Does Rain Fall?

With no wind driving it, rain falls between 5 and 20 mph, depending upon the size of the raindrop. Drizzle is composed of molecules of water so small that they practically float on air. These drops will fall much more slowly than the larger raindrops.

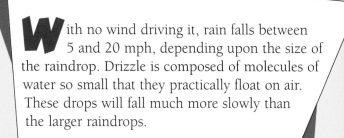

The Water Cycle:

Earth's water goes through an endless cycle of evaporation (water changing into vapor and rising into the air) and condensation (vapor changing back to water and falling as precipitation).

No Picnicking:

The rainiest place on earth is Mt. Waialeale (Wi **aw**lee **aw**lee) on the island of Kauai, Hawaii, with up to 350 rainy days a year. This amounts to an average rainfall of 460 inches per year. Mt. Waialeale is one of the most scenic mountains in the world. It is emerald green with white cascading waterfalls on all sides, and usually a halo of clouds.

Ask Max!

Just for the Record:

Hail is a piece of ice that comes from a thunderstorm. **Sleet** is frozen rain. **Freezing rain** is rain that freezes when it lands on a surface that has a temperature below freezing.

Freezing Rain — 36° / 34° / 33° / 32° / 31° / 30°

Sleet — 34° / 32° / 31° / 30° / 30° / 30°

Snow — 28° / 29° / 30° / 31° / 31° / 30°

A Long Dry Spell:

The Bible records many droughts. One drought of three and a half years was caused by the prayer of the faithful prophet, Elijah. Another prayer by Elijah also ended the drought (James 5:17,18). In modern times, Arica, Chile went the longest length of time with no rain: from October 1903 to January 1918 — over 14 years!

Icy Desert:

Antarctica gets less precipitation than any other continent on earth and can technically be classified as a desert.

What is the shape of a raindrop?

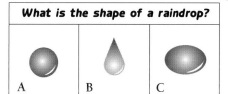

A   B   C

Artists have given most people the impression that **B** is the shape of a raindrop. This is not accurate. Small raindrops look like **A**, spherical; large raindrops look like **C**, more like a hamburger bun.

The average speed of a tornado along the ground is about 35 mph, and actual speed may range from 20 to 60 mph. The width of a tornado may be anywhere from 50 yards to over a mile wide, and the path averages a distance of around four miles. The speed of the wind within a tornado funnel can exceed 300 mph, allowing it to lift houses off foundations, sling automobiles through the air, and snap huge trees at their trunks.

Tornado Alley

Where the Wind Comes Sweepin' Down the Plain:

No state is "tornado-less," but tornadoes appear most often in the central United States in an area known as "tornado alley" extending through the states of Texas, Oklahoma, Kansas, and Nebraska.

cool dry air

cool dry air

warm cool air

The Formation of a Tornado

Strange and Amazing Tornado Effects:

• Broom straws have been found imbedded in the trunks of trees.

• Chickens have commonly been found stripped of their feathers.

• In the Great Bend, Kansas tornado of November, 1915, an entire farm was destroyed, but five horses that had been hitched to a rail inside of a barn were found a quarter of a mile away, unharmed, still hitched to the rail.

• One of the deadliest tornadoes in history hit St. Louis, Missouri in May of 1896. A sleeping man was picked up by the twister along with his mattress and bedding, and deposited unharmed over a quarter of a mile away.

Chances Are:

Three of every four tornadoes in the world occur in the United States.

Make Your Own Tornado!

You'll need:

• Two 2-liter plastic bottles with labels removed
• Duct tape
• Water

1. Fill one of the bottles about $\frac{3}{4}$ full with water.

2. Put the empty bottle on top of the bottle filled with water, with the openings aligned and touching.

3. Tape the bottles together around the openings. Make sure that no water will leak out.

4. Holding the bottles by the necks, turn the bottles over and rotate them in a circular motion until a tornado starts to form.

5. After some water is in the bottom bottle for balance, set the bottles upright, and let go.

6. Watch the tornado spin out of the top bottle into the bottom.

7. For more color, try adding some drink mix or food coloring.

What Causes Rainbows?

In order to see a rainbow, you must have the sun behind you and be looking toward water drops in the air, usually in the form of rain. Sunlight contains every color, but we see sunlight as white light, until it is reflected (bounced back) or refracted (bent). In the case of the rainbow, a ray of sunlight enters a drop of water, refracts, and then reflects off of the opposite surface of the drop and exits at the front, refracting again as it exits. As it exits the drop of water, the ray of sunlight spreads into the different colors that we call the spectrum. That's the basic answer. It gets more technical from here.

Colorful Covenant:

Rainbows were first seen by Noah and his family immediately after the Flood as God used the rainbow to symbolize His covenant with Noah that He would never again destroy the earth with a flood (Gen. 9:8-17).

Sunlight

Raindrop

Ask Max!

Make a Rainbow!

You'll need:

- Water hose connected to a hydrant
- Sprayer for the end of the hose
- Sunny day

Put the sprayer on the end of the hose, stand with your back to the sun, and spray a steady mist into the air in front of you. You should see a rainbow forming on the mist. If you don't see one at first, try shifting positions with your line of vision and the stream of water until you do.

The Better Half:

A rainbow would be a full circle, if it were not for the ground cutting off the bottom half. Some people in airplanes have seen full "rainbow circles."

Blue Moonbow of Kentucky:

Rainbows don't have to have sunlight to occur. "Moonbows" occur when light from a full moon is bright enough. Kentucky's Cumberland Falls makes a moonbow on a clear night. The park's web site claims that it is the only waterfall in the Western Hemisphere where this phenomenon occurs.

Is It Ever Too Cold to Snow?

I t is never too cold to snow. There is always some moisture in the air. Cold fronts generally bring clear weather and that makes us think that it is too cold to snow.

Too Warm to Snow?

As long as the temperature in the clouds is 32° F or less, snow may fall. It is not unusual for snow to fall when the ground temperature is in the forties.

A Little Chilly for Grass Skirts:

Only one state has never recorded a temperature below zero degrees Fahrenheit — Hawaii. Its lowest temperature so far has been 12° F. Hawaii is also the southernmost of the 50 states.

how can fall
om clear skies
when tempera-
tures are in the
single digits or
colder.

How's the Weather Up There?

If you like wind, cold, and snow, then 6,288-foot
Mt. Washington in New Hampshire is the place for
you. The average wind speed here of 35.4 mph is the
strongest in the United States. The U.S. record for
the strongest surface wind is 231 mph recorded here
in 1934. The record low here is -47° F. The average
daily low for the year is 19.8° F. Wind chills can be
-150° F. The average yearly snowfall is 254 inches.
The ground is permanently frozen in a layer from
20 to 100 feet below the surface on
the summit of this highest mountain
in New Hampshire.

No Deep Breathing Allowed:

In Eastern Siberia, the temperature may plunge
to -90° F. At this extremely low temperature, a
person's breath will immediately turn to ice in
midair and fall to the ground. But don't
inhale to replace that breath. The incoming
air will frost the lungs.

Olly, Olly Oxen Freeze!

Water does not always freeze at
32° F. For water to freeze at this
temperature, it must be still and
shallow. At -40° F, all water will
freeze. If you tossed water from
a bucket out the door at that
temperature, it would freeze
before it hit the ground.

Give 'Em an Inch . . .

An inch of ice is heavier than an inch of
snow. On the average, an inch of rain is
equivalent to ten inches of snow.

Lightning is a powerful current of electricity flowing through a thin channel of charged air. As the lightning flows through this space, it heats the air to a temperature of 18,000 to 54,000° F — hotter than the surface of the sun. The super-heated air expands violently, and contracts instantaneously, creating a shockwave that produces the sound waves we know as thunder.

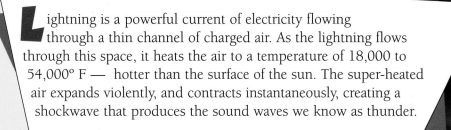

Tropical Target:

More thunderstorms – 3,000 a day – hit the tropics than any other place on earth. That's because there is more warm, moist air there. This air is sucked up into a large cloud where it condenses, making the cloud grow larger and "mushroom shaped." The cloud will continue growing until it is full of violent winds, water, electricity, and ice — all the ingredients for a thunderstorm.

A. Electrical charges build up in the cloud.

B. Leader stroke discharges to the ground.

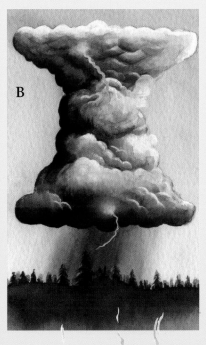

C. Return stroke flashes back up to the cloud. The air expands with a clap of thunder.

Supercharged Spaghetti!

The average lightning bolt is only about an inch in diameter, but the average length is about six miles.

Automatic Flash:

Lightning strikes the earth 100 times every second.

Dead Ringer:

For centuries in Europe, superstitious people thought that lightning was sent by evil spirits to destroy churches. Someone would be sent to the church to ring the bells to scare away the evil spirits. Often, lightning would strike the bell tower, sending as much as 100 million volts of electricity down the ropes to the bell-ringer. Hundreds of bell-ringers were killed before the practice was outlawed.

Public Enemy Number 1:

More people are killed by lightning each year in the United States than floods, hurricanes, or tornadoes.

Printed in the United States of America

Please visit our web site for other great titles:
www.masterbooks.net